Better
Keep it
in the
Notes

PALMETTO
P U B L I S H I N G
Charleston, SC
www.PalmettoPublishing.com

Copyright © 2024 by Leslie Lauren

All rights reserved
No portion of this book may be reproduced, stored in a retrieval system, or transmitted in any form by any means–electronic, mechanical, photocopy, recording, or other–except for brief quotations in printed reviews, without prior permission of the author.

Paperback ISBN: 9798822959675

Better Keep it in the Notes

LESLIE LAUREN

Contents

Summer rain chronicles Part 1	1
Manifesting	3
Bones of the skull	5
Jealousy	7
Recipes	9
Summer Rain Chronicles Part 2	12
Teddy bear	14
Coffee shop	16
10 years	18
Translation 1	20
Influenza	22
Love	24
O - kay	26
Adjusting	28
Manifesting 2	30
summer rain chronicles Part 3	32
I wish I was just visiting	35
Strangers	37

Translation 2	40
Target Run	42
White-shirt	44
The 30's Diagnosis	47
Warning!	49
Drafts of the letters I was going to send	51
movies i want to watch	55
My future vows	56
Missing Assignments	58
Songs that inspired this book	60
Thank you for reading	62
Acknowledgments	63

Thank you to all

Summer rain chronicles
Part 1

Feeling sensational, heard, comfortable, safe. Aesthetically pleasing is hard to feel with or without someone but in this moment I feel everything. Everything is possible sitting in my cream-colored chair with pink flamingos, and wooden legs. Planted on my desk, is a book, my computer, and a guitar with one broken string. It's summer, the house is filled with dense air and moisture from the rain. It feels like a warm hug, a needed hug, a type of hug that is needed after a long slow day, or the type of warmth that is only felt with someone's hug. The warmth of that hug lasts forever when you believe in it. Coursing through your body and heals your heart like medicine, curing a minor cold during flu season.

up to down

left to you were also right

warmth and coldness

Cold, I feel cold with no warmth, I feel no warmth, I feel no love, and what am I with no love? but at this very moment, I have the summer rain to thank for the love and warmth. I love myself

Manifesting

I am wealthy

I am abundant

I am a millionaire

I am valuable

I am a money Magnet

I am rich

Bones of the skull

Neurocranium - is a cast formed around the brain. It is made up of eight parts: Frontal, sphenoid, ethmoid, occipital, 2 temporal, and 2 parietal bones

Jealousy

When Kendall Jenner caught the eyes of every boy in my 3-grade class in 2015, all the girls were jealous. They wanted to be her, be the girl wanted by their crush. One of them asked me if I was jealous, I said yes, I was jealous but not of Kendall Jenner. I was jealous of people who were buried 6 feet underground.

Recipes

Mac and cheese

4 1/2 cups of heavy cream

4 oz of cream cheese 1 small onion 6 cloves of minced garlic 1 stick of unsalted butter

(The recipe is not even finished, and I never made it)

Summer Rain Chronicles
Part 2

I miss the summer rain, I want summer rain, I need summer rain. I am so cold without it, I am 32 degrees too cold. I need my warmth; Warmth provides me with a healed body, and coldness gives me stillness and a running nose. When I was younger I had so much natural warmth that I didn't even need to be bundled up to face the coldness. Now I feel like I need those eyes to watch the path ahead of me, catch me before I go crashing into the fence of that house I loved. come back to me summer rain

I love you

Teddy bear

Saying this is so funny that I could ball my eyes out for weeks, and throw up every time I think of him, okay here goes everything

He used to look for me and smile when I walked in the room. Now he looks at me, but only to pass the time or wait for me to pass through the door to look for anybody else.

Coffee shop

Matcha iced lattes taste like grass
Literature is boring, guess that is the reason women choose cliterature.
A man screaming at the cashier because he wants a plain black coffee
Another man stomping steps shakes my table and grassy drink
A woman pushing the table close to her, to strap her in like a roller coaster
okay

        1

              2

                    3

Feet together, rise up, and snapshot This lady just took a picture of her feet, to be fair she
had shoes on
But
Great heavens
The great thing about writing and minding your business is you can do it anywhere and all the time or when something piques your interest, write like it's your business.

10 years

10 years is a long time

10 whole years

120 months

521 weeks

3652 days

87,648 hours and

Even bigger numbers for minutes and seconds in 10 years.

So why did we waste it? we had time we had chances you could've grabbed my hand when you were drowning but instead, you took a chance at dying knowing well that you were not strong enough to save yourself or anyone or maybe you were?

I guess I will never forget the 10 years you wasted for you not to grab my hand and the next 10 preparing myself to save you again

Translation 1

Informal way

    Salt, je m'appelle Leslie, Enchantee dete renconter

Translation:

    Hi. I'm Leslie, Nice to meet you

s

Influenza

Influenza

They assumed that its origins is from Camp fusion

They thought it was the normal flu

It was different then the common flu because the spreading pace was fast
        It started in Boston in Oct. It spread to the whole nation

Symptoms - just like the flu at first

then as time goes on painful headaches, very high fevers, pain in joints and muscles, and trouble breathing. Finally the filling of the lungs *love*

If I find him, I am complete

or

I am dead

O - kay

I don't like touch, I feel sick when my mother comes close to me, and I hear her breathe out and onto my skin.

It hurts to be touched when not wanted, but it hurts more when it's "because I love you". It's massaging deep tissue in my grandma's fragile bones, touched and touching her neck, shoulders, and back.

After I tell her that I am done, she complains that I didn't do well enough and says "can you do it again".

And my answer has to be just: "okay".

Adjusting

when I met you, I was adjusting
when I was with you, I was adjusting and
Now that I am without you I am justifying something that
I should have known to be disgust but again I was adjusting.
Adjusting to your ways and actions, when it was your turn, became my problem. Lifting a finger to swipe right, but not your ass to help with a small load of anything.
But I guess I can't complain and rage about you, I Loved you with a blindfold.

                I still loved something of you

So I am adjusting to the light,
to empty space,
to cold weather,
to blank stares,
adjusting. I think I am having a hard time adjusting.

Manifesting 2

I am wealthy

I am abundant

I am millionaire

I am available

I am a money magnet

I attract money

I am rich

summer rain chronicles
Part 3

Summer rain never come again

Never rain again

Never ever look at me like that again, like you don't know me like you don't care if I was somebody else.

I looked at you and I gave you me and you gave me right back in my face because suddenly you formed cold and reflective. I looked at you with ease to help you release, l talked to you softly and quietly because I talk too loud and you needed comfort and love like the motherly type. So I gave to you, I sat, I listened, I waited. What will you do?

I kneeled, you smirked, I bent over, you pushed, I gave, you took. And for what? For you to show me a lesson? Finally, teach me the things you thought I wasn't ready for. The major thunderstorms? The dense heat? The high winds?

Anyway, the season is ending so your stormy clouds will clear, and down you'll fall with the leaves of the new season, you never understood right?

Right

Well you're just a man who thinks like a child and I am a child who is afraid of men, so I am not afraid of you.

And now we mourn all the self-righteousness and respect I had left in me before I met you, yes I was already broken, you should have known. You met me in a place people call hell on earth. And I should have known I was still in hell when I didn't feel different, I was just walking into another part of hell your personal hell made for me. But if I were a woman,I would give you hell right back.

I hate you

I wish I was just visiting

I hate Chicago. It's a dry, less trash, rat-infested city than New York. But only people who have fun are the people who love Chicago sports, people who visit Chicago on vacation, people who love being the "hottest" guy in the bar with no girl or care in the world about anything else but looking good.

Strangers

Why do we fall in love with strangers?

Is it the way they speak or dress that catches our eyes or how they present themselves to you, the way they seem so different and mesmerizing just by looking at them amongst the people?

Creating scenarios in your head on what their life is like imagining why would two different pieces of two different puzzles fit together and why they curiosity fit or maybe it just shows that you are a very observational person and you notice everyone in the room when others don't or you are a person who is so desperate for love that romanticizing about a relationship with a somewhat good looking person and setting for anyone that you again don't know.

Why does a random stranger make me feel like this after so long?

I don't know him on any type of level not even personally

I don't know his name, his birthday, or his social security number

Just a guy on the train

He was wearing white retro sneakers that were a little worn out, white long socks light blue wash jeans a greenish blue puffy jacket but underneath he wore a white turtleneck shirt, for character he had a brown leather watch that about every five minutes or so he checked it but played it off like he was adjusting it at one point he fully took it off just to put it back on I'd like to Imagine it's his grandpa's watch that he got when he was a little kid but never could wear because it was big on his wrist, and today he tried it on and it fit for the first time so he wore it. It is in honor of his grandpa. He also had a newspaper stuffed in his back pocket, and a flip phone which I thought was weird considering that the year was 2016, not 2006 but oddly enough it made me still feel attracted to him. He was blonde with dark blue eyes I don't know but something about him was the most interesting thing I have ever seen and the last thing I have ever wanted to learn more about.

The last time I laid my eyes on his was when he got out of the train car and walked away

Translation 2

French words

comment allez - vous = how are you
bien = good
je m'appelle = My name is
enchante = pleased to meet you
Le francais = french
je suis = I am
vous = you
bonne journee = have a good day
bonjour = hello
mademoiselle = miss
oui = yes

Target Run

- AirPods case
- body mist
- And a book

White-shirt

Why is every guy on the street wearing white shirts? No, really I swear about 10 guys are wearing white shirts, like mean girls but bro code for "white shirts = casual and comfy, comfort for the guy in the clothes and casual for in case Ryan Reynolds is there" plus a nod for when they see another guy in a white shirt.

is it wear a white shirt and get free beer at any bar in Chicago probably

Or is it a sign it's time for me to go, is this tall white guy in a white shirt guy supposed to symbolize a white dove? but my kind of symbolic truth is that I don't belong here.

A woman passes by with what I am guessing is her husband and son as soon as I typed "symbolic" she said "it symbolizes " but got confused in thought and said instead "it's by the holy church you go to" saying to her son, him just listening because he doesn't care about what his mother was saying he doesn't laugh a little bit or give his mom the okay I get it he just listened to what she was saying and moved on.

She laughed at her own words at the end of the block

Another white shirt white guy passed by, am I missing something?

It's 11:13 at night. I should be in bed and dreaming of going to school in the morning but I am here sitting outside of the closed Starbucks where memories started and ended, replaying in silence for eternity. memories as old as eternity must really suck to be eternity to live in those memories. I start listening to the music again not tuning it out, like that man listening to his wife talking and giving her the best "I give fuck" face that he pulled out of the square pocket of his white shirt-

Oh his white shirt

Another guy passed by but he has a shirt on that was not white or close to white it was blue

Maybe the reason for today was to wear a white shirt and get free beer, but I think I just noticed every guy wearing a white shirt because of you

The 30's Diagnosis

Why is it I chose the older man, there are boys my age. There's more in common with boys but with men there's tension. The eyes, the knee touch, the guiding, it's all imanaive. It's the power balance, the forbidden, the perfect relapse after you have been clean. He's not the first and at this point won't be the last. My head is feeling a bit warm, sorry about that

ooh, My face is heated

                                      My tears start to spill

I skip a heartbeat, now my skewed breath is screwing my words and mind

I think I am getting sick

Warning!

My ears hurt but it's okay I deserve it, I deserve it. I want to take off my headphones but I can't. At low volume to the maximum.

The music is going into my ears and not coming out. It stays within me and lingers when the hurt is over, soothing the aftermath.

Drafts of the letters I was going to send

Did you ever think about me

                                        And then you just ghost

Like you did in those plays you used to do

I still have the love letters that you wrote me sometime age

movies i want to watch

- The hot chick

My future vows

Everything is white, it is so predictable and dark. It's like I am not even using my brain to put effort into it. it's lazy, not thought out, and sounds unmeaningful. So what am I supposed to write when I need to write a letter to a college when I apply for college or when my husband and I get married, I need vows. What am I supposed to say " Dear (insert name of future husband) I love you and that's all I got, enjoy the cake everyone"

Missing Assignments

- Personality quiz
- Foraging society
- types of claims theme in "La luna "

  + 100 more missing assignments

Songs that inspired this book

Labor - Paris Paloma
Let the Light In - Lana del Ray
Sinner - The last dinner party
Love myself - Hailee Steinfeld
Tame Impala - cause I'm a Man
Wildest Dreams - Taylor Swift
Vampire - Olivia Rodrigo
Normal Fucking Rockwell - Lana Del Ray
Down Bad - Taylor Swift
under/over - Gracie Abrams
would've, Could've, should've - Taylor Swift
We can't be friends - Ariana Grande
It's possible - Piero Piccioni, Catherine Howe
I'll be seeing you - Billie Holiday
Killing me softly - Fugees
Who's Afraid of Little old me? - Taylor Swift
Francis Forever - Mitski
Glory Box - Portishead
F2020 - Avenue Beat
Love affair - UMI

Thank you for reading

Acknowledgments

Milton Keynes UK
Ingram Content Group UK Ltd.
UKHW020752051024
449151UK00012B/545